Book-Write

BOOK-WRITE

A Creative Bookmaking Guide
For Young Authors

Michelle O'Brien-Palmer

illustrations
Shannon Rubin

MicNik Publications

Credits

Illustrations:	Shannon Rubin
Educational Consultant:	Shannon Rubin
Cover Design:	Denny Driver
Cover Photography:	Lance O. Kenyon
Computer Assistance:	Tom Radcliffe
Publishing Editor:	Laura Utterback
Content Editors:	Eileen Gibbons, teacher, Rochester, NY
	Harriet Herman, parent, Bellevue, WA
	Marci Larsen, principal, North Bend, WA
	Robert O'Brien, author, Rochester, NY
	Nicholas Palmer, 2nd grade student, Woodinville, WA
	Brandon Schnierer, 4th grade student, Woodinville, WA
Young Authors:	Terry Yoo, 1st grader
	Steven Yoo, 1st grader
	Nick Palmer, 2nd grader
	Brandon Schnierer, 4th grader
	Jessica Ruble, 5th grader
	Brigida Swanson, 6th grader

ISBN 1-879235-01-3
Library of Congress Catalog Card Number: 91-68412
Copyright © 1992 Michelle O'Brien-Palmer

Manufactured in the United States of America

10 9 8 7 6 5 4 3

ATTENTION: SCHOOLS AND BUSINESSES

Books from MicNik Publications are available at quantity discounts with bulk purchase for educational, business, or sales promotional use. For information, please write to:
MicNik Publications
P.O. Box 3041, Kirkland, WA 98072
(206) 881-6476

The Young Author

The writing process is a mystical, magical and wonderfully creative adventure. One starts with countless possibilities - all pre-writing ideas waiting to be heard. Then one special idea comes to life when written on paper in the first draft. As the author molds her work in revision, she continues to paint her picture with words. In editing her masterpiece she makes her work sparkle for her soon-to-be audience. Then she proudly presents her special, published, one-of-a-kind creation, in book form.

She has painted a picture with words. She has sculpted her story on paper. She is a creative and truly talented young author: a sight for all to behold!

Michelle

Acknowledgements

Many special people have contributed to making this book a reality. I would like to thank them for their encouragement and support. This book is a culmination of our collective vision.

I am especially grateful to my friend, illustrator, and educational consultant – Shannon Rubin. She has been my touchstone; a truly critical player in the creation of this book. Her inspired illustrations and guidance helped breathe joy and life into the text.

I also extend sincere thanks to those who helped in the production of this book:

To the young authors for their wonderful stories and illustrations – Terry and Steven Yoo, Brandon Schnierer, Brigida Swanson, Jessica Ruble and Nicholas Palmer.

To my content editors for their dedication to this project even though editing took place on almost all of the major holidays – Eileen Gibbons, Harriet Herman, Marci Larsen, Robert O'Brien, Nick Palmer, and Brandon Schnierer.

To Ray Sevin of Bookcrafters for his guidance and support in this project, to Laura Utterback for her professional editing support, to Lance O. Kenyon for his delightful cover photo and to Denny Driver for his wonderful cover design.

Last, but not least, I wish to thank my best friend – my husband, Gid Palmer. Thank you for your belief in this project, for your never-ending support and for picking up the slack at home. I couldn't have written this without you.

Dedication

In loving memory of my grandmother, Marjorie Ballou Dawson.
She taught me to believe in myself and to do what I love.

Table of Contents

Introduction
for parents and teachers

BOOK-WRITE is written to help young authors (Pre-6) experience the joy and exhilaration of creating their own unique books. Non-writers are not exempt from this process. With your help in dictation or with their illustrations alone, they too can experience the wonder of bookmaking.

One of the goals of BOOK-WRITE is to empower the young author. It is written to promote the author's investment and ownership in his creation. The bookmaking decisions belong to each author. Among other decisions, they will determine what they want to write, when they are satisfied with their text and what type of book they want to make. BOOK-WRITE takes a young author from the idea stage through the actual bookmaking process using other young authors' writing as examples. Although the text speaks to the young author directly, it will require adult supervision and guidance in most cases.

Many chapters include a page defining the main topic and a page giving information about their contents. Whenever more information might be helpful to parents or teachers it will be found in italics just under the top border of a text page. A glossary is included to define any unfamiliar words. There is a chapter of forms for you to use with your young authors. Make as many copies of these forms as you need. The resource chapter at the end of the book is intended to provide information regarding some publishers of children's writing and a list of excellent reference books for bookmaking and writing with young authors.

Each idea in this book is meant to be taken as liberally as possible. There is no one right way to do anything. The more variations created, the more exciting the process will be.

Guide, watch and experience the creative wonder of each of our precious young authors!

Foreword

Note to Young Authors

I am an author and an illustrator. If you have ever written, drawn or told a story, you are an author too. If you have drawn a picture, you are also an illustrator.

As a fellow author, I have been invited to visit many classrooms and to read the young authors' books. Each book was different and very special. I loved reading them.

In talking with young authors I've learned that we really have a lot in common. Many of them use the same writing process that I do to create their books. They enjoy writing this way as much as I do. I wrote this book to share what I know about book-writing with you. I hope you have fun writing your own books too!

Chapter 1

5 Step Writing Process

Introduction to the 5 Step Writing Process

This chapter provides a brief introduction to each step of the writing process. For more detailed information please see the actual chapter. As BOOK-WRITE guides you through the five step writing process it will follow the progress of six young authors. Their names, grade levels and book titles are listed below:

Terry Yoo	1st grade student	<u>My Journal</u>
Steven Yoo	1st grade student	<u>Hilda, the Wich</u>
Nick Palmer	2nd grade student	<u>The Husky Game</u>
Brandon Schnierer	4th grade student	<u>A First Place Team</u>
Jessica Ruble	5th grade student	<u>Dolphins</u>
Brigida Swanson	6th grade student	<u>Sari Goes to School</u>

Step 1: Pre-Writing

Pre-writing means before-writing. In this step you think through what you want to write about, why you want to write this book and who you want to read it. Many authors have an idea list that they keep with them so any time they think of a new book idea they can write it down. It helps them to have lots of ideas from which to choose.

Step 2: Drafting

In drafting you take your pre-writing ideas and put them onto paper. The goal is to just get your words down. You don't pay attention to spelling or punctuation. Drafts are very exciting. Your book is coming to life.

Step 3: Revision

In revision you re-read your draft and ask yourself and your reader questions about the content of your writing. Does it say what I want it to say? Does my reader understand what I've said? Do I want to add more information? You are fine-tuning your creation in revision.

Step 4: Editing

In editing you check your draft for spelling, punctuation and grammar changes. As in revision, it really helps to have someone else read your writing for errors too. All authors do this because it is very hard to find your own mistakes. Editors are really important in the bookmaking process. Once your draft is edited you are very close to presenting it to your audience.

Step 5: Publishing

In publishing you make a book ready to present to its audience. It is an exciting step. You will decide the type of book you will make. You will re-write your revised and edited draft into your final copy. (Chapter 7, Books To Make, will show you how to make six different types of books.) You will make the special pages found in a published book. But, most importantly, you will present your published book to its audience. It is a time to be very proud. Your books will bring joy to you the rest of your life.

The 5 Step Writing Process outlined in this book is one that has worked well for many young authors. However, there is no one right way to use it. There is your way– that's the right way for you.

Some young authors really find pre-writing helpful; others use the pre-writing checklist to determine their audience and purpose and go straight to their draft. That's OK! Some young authors write three or four drafts, revising and editing each one until they feel satisfied enough to re-write their final draft into a published copy. Other young authors are satisfied writing one or two drafts.

This is your book. You are the author. You make the choices throughout the writing process that determine the shape and form of your creation. You decide when you feel ready to share it with your audience.

Chapter 2
Pre-Writing

Pre-Writing Defined

"The author starts out with countless possibilities – all pre-writing ideas waiting to be heard..."

Pre-writing is the first step in the writing process. It happens before your book writing begins. Pre-writing can help you to create writing ideas and ways to plan out your story. It helps you to identify why you are writing (purpose) and who you want to read your book (audience).

Pre-writes can take on many forms. They can be written, illustrated, tape recorded, or played out as a drama. In this chapter there are many pre-writing ideas (techniques) for you to explore. To make each pre-write even more exciting take a look at the "Just for Fun" section or make your own changes.

The sky is your limit. Pre-writing should be a fun and exciting process. ***Enjoy yourself!***

About This Chapter

This chapter includes...

A Pre-Writing Checklist

The **Pre-Writing Checklist** on page 12 is designed to help you decide upon your writing purpose and audience. This checklist stays with you during the writing process.

Writing Idea Sheets

Authors come up with their writing ideas in many different ways. This chapter shows two simple ways for you to create your writing topics. (Choose one)

Pre-Writing Techniques

Once you have your topic, you might want to use a pre-writing technique to think through your story before writing your draft. You can use your own technique or one below:

Pre-Writing Checklist Ingredients

This checklist can be used by all writers. A non-writer can dictate his answers.

Materials:

Pre-writing checklist (copy – page 105)
Pencil/pen

Goals:

To decide why you are writing (purpose)
To decide who the reader will be (audience)
To choose a pre-writing idea
To write down your topic

Steps:

1. Place a checkmark next to your answers in the first two questions.
2. Look through the pre-writing techniques in this chapter to determine your answers in question 3.
3. Answer the last question after you have used a technique to determine your topic.
4. Keep your checklist with you during the writing process to remind you of your purpose and audience.

Pre-Writing Checklist Example

Pre-Writing Checklist

Purpose

Why...
do you want to write your book?

- ☑ I want to tell a story
- ◯ I'm writing a report
- ◯ Just for fun
- ◯ Write your own reason:

Audience

Who...
do you want to read your book?

- ☑ Friend
- ☑ Parent
- ◯ Grandparent
- ◯ Brother
- ◯ Sister
- ◯ Teacher
- ◯ Librarian
- ◯ Others:

Pre-Writing Technique

Which...
technique would you like to use?

to determine your topic...
- ◯ Brainstorming
- ☑ Idea List

to think before you write...
- ◯ Picture Story
- ☑ Four Square W's
- ◯ Story Map
- ◯ Idea Chart
- ◯ Report
- ◯ Other:

Topic

What...
topic did you decide upon?

Husky game

My Name is: _Nick_   Date: _10-15-91_

Idea List Ingredients

The idea list helps young authors to select their topic from a list of things they really want to write about.

Materials:
Form (copy – page 106)
Pencil/pen/markers

Goals:
To create ideas for future writing
To continue listing new ideas

Steps:
1. Write down things you want to write about.
2. Keep your list handy so you can write new ideas as you think of them.
3. Check off each completed writing stage.

Just for Fun:
Use large newsprint and tape ideas to a wall
Use a small sheet for your wallet or pocket
Use colored/shaped paper

Ongoing Idea List Example

Name: Nick

Things I want to write about

	Pre-Write	Draft	Revision	Edit	Publish
Nintendo	✓	✓	✓	✓	✓
My family	✓	✓	✓		
Sissy the cat					
Soccer game					
my Grandparents					
knots bery farm	✓	✓			
Husky game	✓	✓	✓	✓	✓

Brainstorming Ingredients

Brainstorming is a fun way for authors of all ages to create their own writing ideas. Non-writers can dictate their ideas.

Materials:
Form (copy – page 107)
Pencil/pen/markers

Goal:
To list as many writing ideas as you can

Steps:
1. Write your ideas in the clouds or around the idea bolt.
2. Use your ideas for future books.

Just for Fun:
Create your own form with different shapes
Use large paper and hang it on a wall
Write as quickly as you can

Brainstorming Example

Name: _John_

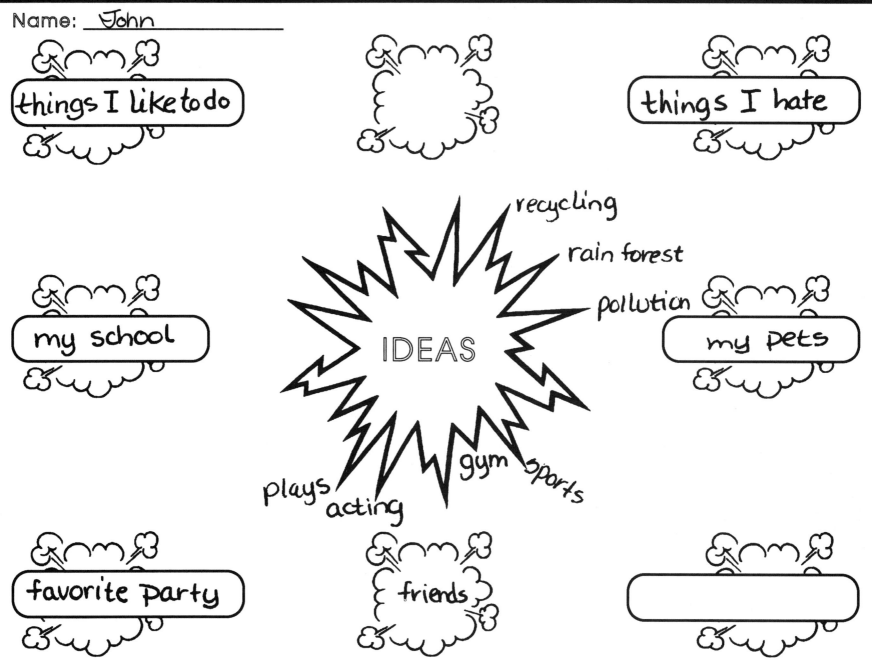

things I like to do

things I hate

my school

IDEAS

recycling

rain forest

pollution

my pets

plays acting

gym sports

favorite party

friends

Picture Story Ingredients

Fun for all ages but especially great for non-writers. Some young authors will feel finished after drawing their pictures and others will want to accompany the drawings with words.

Materials:

Paper

Pencil/pens/markers/crayons

Goal:

To create a story with pictures

Step:

1. Draw one picture or a group of pictures that tell your story.

Just for Fun:

Cut out paper shapes and draw on them

Draw on butcher paper

Draw on paper plates

Draw to music

Picture Story Pre-Write Example

Four Square W's Ingredients

Non-writers can dictate their answers. The topic can come from the author's idea list or brainstorming sheet. The four square technique helps authors with early character and plot development.

Materials:
Form (copy – page 108)
Pencil/pen/markers

Goal:
To think through your story

Steps:
1. Write in your topic.
2. Answer the questions in each square.

Just for Fun:
Add more squares and questions
Use different shapes for questions
Cut question shapes and arrange them
  into story form
Use puppets to answer the questions
Tape record your answers

Four Square W's Pre-Write Example

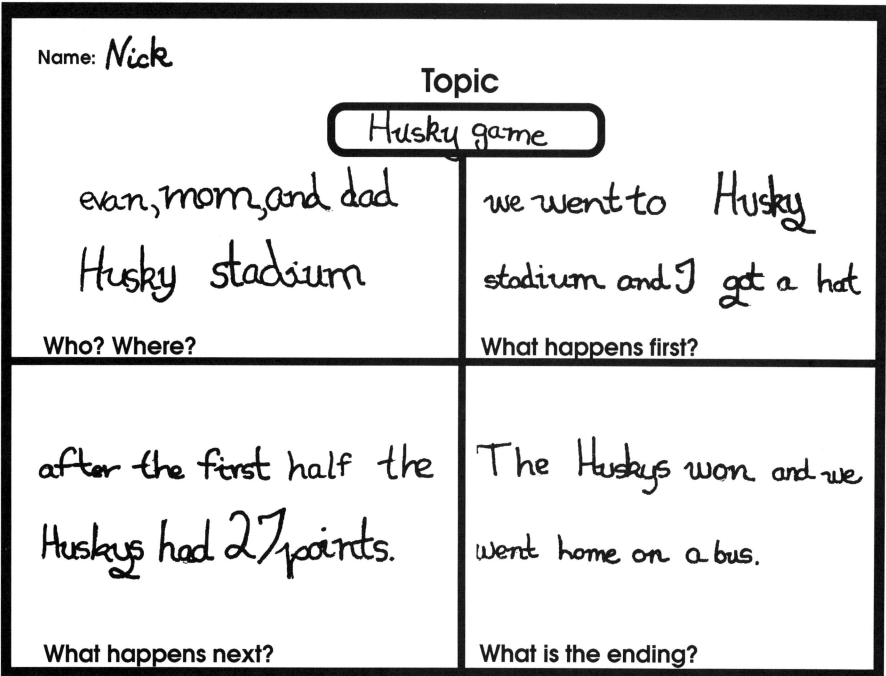

Name: Nick

Topic

Husky game

evan, mom, and dad
Husky stadium

Who? Where?

we went to Husky
stadium and I got a hat

What happens first?

after the first half the
Huskys had 27 points.

What happens next?

The Huskys won and we
went home on a bus.

What is the ending?

Idea Chart Ingredients

The idea chart helps young authors to build upon their main topic. They place sub-topics in the different shapes and can also include what their characters saw, heard and felt. Some young authors will keep this form simple and others will make it very complex.

Materials:
Form (copy – page 109)
Pencil/pen/markers

Goals:
To spin off ideas from the main idea
To map out different parts of the story

Steps:
1. Write your main topic in the large shape.
2. Write related ideas in the small shapes.
3. Write even more information under the lines.

Just For Fun:
Use butcher paper/colored paper
Make each shape a different color

Idea Chart Pre-Write Example

Name: Nick

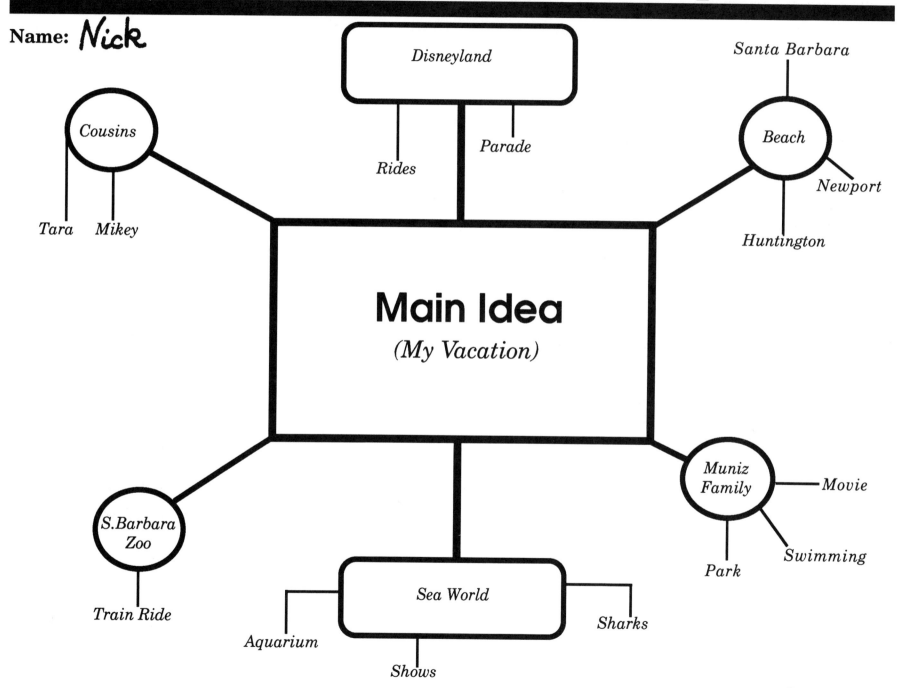

Disneyland
- Rides
- Parade

Cousins
- Tara
- Mikey

Beach
- Santa Barbara
- Newport
- Huntington

Main Idea
(My Vacation)

S.Barbara Zoo
- Train Ride

Sea World
- Aquarium
- Shows
- Sharks

Muniz Family
- Movie
- Swimming
- Park

Story Map Ingredients

Story mapping helps more advanced young authors to focus on developing their story characters, setting, plot and conclusion.

Materials:
Form (copy – page 110)
Pencil/pen/markers

Goal:
To map your story before you start writing

Steps:
1. Who do I want my story to be about? (Main character)
2. Who else do I want in my story? (Supporting characters)
3. Where do I want them to be? (Setting)
4. What do I want to have happen? (Plot)
5. How will my story end? (Conclusion)

Just for Fun:
Use an easel pad/newsprint
Draw the setting and map the story inside your drawing

Story Map Pre-Write Example

Name: *Brandon*
Story Topic: *First Place Team*

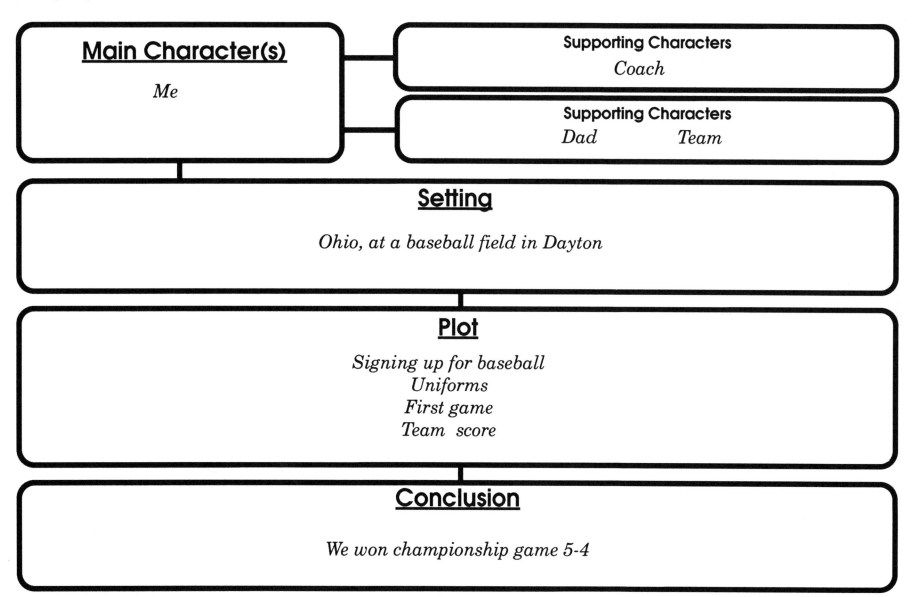

Main Character(s)

Me

Supporting Characters
Coach

Supporting Characters
Dad   *Team*

Setting

Ohio, at a baseball field in Dayton

Plot

Signing up for baseball
Uniforms
First game
Team score

Conclusion

We won championship game 5-4

Report Flow-Chart Ingredients

This flow-chart is used to help a young author form the foundation for his report. Before he writes his first draft he needs to research his topic questions.

Materials:
Form (copy – page 111)
Pencil/pen/markers

Goals:
To decide upon your research questions
To create a flow-chart to help organize your
 report into sections or chapters

Steps:
1. Determine what you want to investigate.
   (Topic)
2. Write down the questions you have about
   your topic. (Research questions)
3. Research each question to determine your
   sub-topics.

Just for Fun:
Create your own form
Write your questions on index cards

Report Flow-Chart Pre-Write Example

Name: *Jessica*
5th Grade

Dolphins

Description
- Blowhole
- Body Structure
- Skin

Intelligence
- Nice
- Trainable
- Caring
- Sea World
- Studies

Communication
- Sonar
- Signal for danger
- Sounds

Fishing Nets
- Caught
- Tuna problem

Questions

How do dolphins communicate?

What are their characteristics?

Are dolphins smart?

What happens with fishing nets?

Chapter 3

Drafting

Drafting Defined

"One special idea comes to life when written on paper in the first draft..."

Drafting is the second step in the writing process. Your pre-write is used to help direct the writing of your draft.

Sometimes a draft is called "sloppy copy" to help the writer relax and write without worrying about spelling, punctuation or sentence structure. It's a time to just get your words onto the paper.

Most authors skip a line when writing their draft. This gives them space to revise and edit later. Some authors revise and re-draft many times before they complete their writing process.

Drafting can be an explosively creative process. You give your words life as they flow onto your paper. ***Have fun!***

About This Chapter

This chapter includes...

A Draft Checklist

The **Draft Checklist** on page 32 helps challenge you to write from a different perspective (voice) or try a new writing form such as poetry or a fairytale. This checklist should be used by young authors experienced in the writing process.

Drafts of Other Young Authors

Draft Example	Author and Grade Level		Page Number
Fast-writing	Brigida	6th	34
Journal	Terry	1st	36
Picture Story	Steven	1st	38
Four Square W's	Nick	2nd	40
Story Map	Brandon	4th	42
Report	Jessica	5th	44

Draft Guidelines: *Most authors follow these basic steps when they write their drafts.*

1. Re-read your pre-write.
2. Skip lines as you quickly write onto the page.
3. Don't worry about spelling.
4. If you can't think of a word just leave a space so you can fill it in later.
5. Don't worry about punctuation or grammar.

Draft Checklist Ingredients

This checklist is designed to challenge the writer to take a new perspective or try a new form of writing.

Materials:
Draft checklist (copy – page 112)
Pencil/pen

Goals:
To re-state your writing topic and audience
To decide upon your writing form
To decide upon your writing voice

Steps:
1. Write your topic and audience on the checklist.
2. Check the box which matches the writing form you want to use.
3. Check the box which matches the writing voice you want to use.

Draft Checklist Example

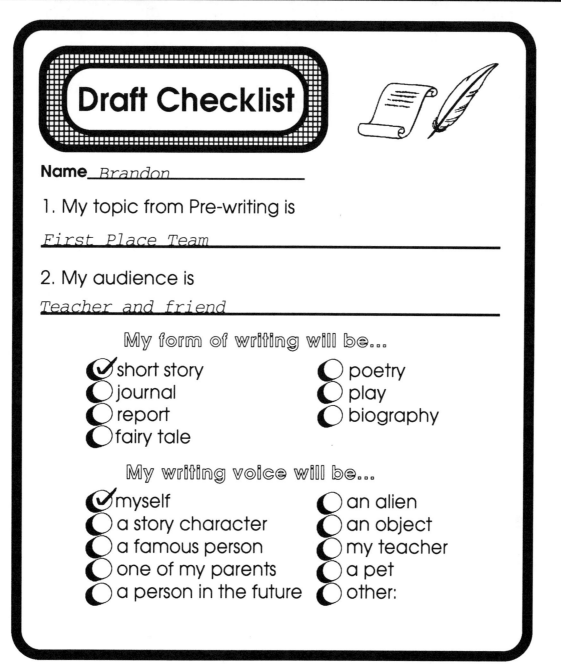

Draft Checklist

Name _Brandon_

1. My topic from Pre-writing is

First Place Team

2. My audience is

Teacher and friend

My form of writing will be...

- ☑ short story
- ◯ journal
- ◯ report
- ◯ fairy tale
- ◯ poetry
- ◯ play
- ◯ biography

My writing voice will be...

- ☑ myself
- ◯ a story character
- ◯ a famous person
- ◯ one of my parents
- ◯ a person in the future
- ◯ an alien
- ◯ an object
- ◯ my teacher
- ◯ a pet
- ◯ other:

Fast-writing Draft Ingredients

This type of writing has been referred to as stream-of-consciousness writing. Whatever comes into the author's mind is written down.

Materials:
Paper
Pencil/pen

Goals:
To write everything that comes into your mind
To just get your words onto your paper

Steps:
1. Write as quickly as you can.
2. Don't worry about spelling or punctuation.

Just for Fun:
Use markers on an easel pad or large paper
Type draft directly onto the computer
Write in a different way; in a circle or sideways

Fast-writing Draft Example

Brigida

  Once there was a little skunk. Her name was Sari. One day she found a backpack. Sari climbed in. All of a sudden it was dark! Someone picked up the backpack and put it on their back. Soon, Sari was asleep. When she woke up, she was in a closet! Luckily, the backpack was open. Sari climbed out and jumped on a shelf. She was very hungry. But look! Over to the left were some small paper bags! Sari walked over to the bags and climbed in one. Yum! The bag had delicious foods in it! Sari had a feast. Sari decided to explore the room outside of the closet. On dear! There are many children sitting at desks! Sari backed up. Suddenly, a bell rang! All of the children ran outside. What luck! Sari walked under the crackand climbed into an open desk. Now there's one thing I should tell you. Never leave your desk opened or a skunk might climb inside. Well, when Sari climbed inside the desk, the teacher said, "Oh Dear, Samantha left her desk opened!" Then she closed her desk. Sari hid behind a watercolor set. When the children came in, they got ready to go home. When Samantha opened her desk she found Sari. Sari ran out of the desk, into the hall and out to the playground. There she found her pleasant family waiting for her. Sari never want into a backpack again.

THE END

(A computer was used to write this draft)

Journal Ingredients

Great for all ages. A journal can include illustrations and different types of writing. A journal can be complete after the draft. However, some authors do go further in the writing process.

Materials:

Lined paper/blank book/spiral notebook
Pencil/pen/crayons/markers

Goal:

To write about things that are important to you

Steps:

1. Decide upon a time of day to write.
2. You can write about your day or something important to you.
3. Don't worry about spelling or punctuation.

Just for Fun:

Make your own special journal and decorate the cover
Draw illustrations in your journal
Start your journal with Today I... or think of your own starting line

Journal Entry Example

in my daddys home

I had a Biday pardy daddy.

we Sang Happy Biday and we

ate a cake.

Picture Story Draft Ingredients

Non-writers can dictate their stories. The writing process can end with the draft. It is up to the young author. If he wants to continue on to the revision process, that's great but not neccessary.

Materials:
Your picture story pre-write
Paper
Pencil/pen

Goal:
To write your story in words

Steps:
1. Look at your pre-write.
2. Write your story onto your paper.
3. Don't worry about spelling or punctuation.

Just for Fun:
Write your draft on computer paper
Cut and paste your drawings onto the paper

Picture Story Draft Example

a Wich Gos up and a Wich sees the moon and

a Wich Sees the Stre and a Wich fulls dewn

Four Square Draft Ingredients

Materials:
Your four square pre-write
Paper
Pencil/pen

Goal:
To write your story

Steps:

1. Look at your pre-write answers.
2. Skipping lines, write your story using your pre-write answers to help you.
3. Don't worry about spelling or punctuation.

Just for Fun:
Use light colored paper
Write with brightly colored pens

Four Square Draft Example

Name: Nick
Date: 10-30-91

    I went to Husky stadiam with

evan, my mom, and my dad we

went there and I got a hot After the first half

the huskies had 27 points. The

Huskies won and we went home on the bus.

Story Map Draft Ingredients

Materials:

Your story map pre-write
Draft checklist (optional)
Paper
Pencil//pen/computer

Goal:

To write your story using the main and
supporting characters, setting, plot and
conclusion from your pre-write

Steps:

1. Re-read your pre-write.
2. Re-read your draft checklist to remind you
   of your story form and voice.
3. Skip lines as you write out your story.
4. Don't worry about spelling or punctuation.

Just for Fun:

Use butcher paper to write your draft

Story Map Draft Example

Brandon
9/12/19

┌─────────────────────┐
│ 1 │ First Place   │
│   │ Team   │
└─────────────────────┘

It was the day the day to sign up for baseball. I was really nervus. I met

my coch "hi Brandon" and talked. Well then I had to get my uneform. Whiel my

dad helped me get in it   we had a praicte and we all did good. By now it

was time for our first game. We got there warmed up, then it was time to PLAY-

BALL1 It started off pretty good we had a eight run inning, they got 0. The

finel score was 15 to 5. By the last game our record was won-16 lost-2. We

were in the championships. It was time for the game. I was really nerves.

Finly we won 5 to 4 we all got a first place trophy we were realy happy.

The Eed

(A computer was used to write this draft)

Report Draft Ingredients

Materials:
Your report flow-chart pre-write
Paper
Pencil/pen/computer

Goal:
To use your flow-chart, research, and notes
to write your draft

Steps:
1. Re-read your pre-write.
2. Skipping lines, write your report using
your pre-write questions and researched
answers.
3. Don't worry about spelling or punctuation.

Report Draft Example

Dolphins: Jessica

You know how dogs talk and they try to talk to each of us? Well dolphins will do that too and other dolphins can understand what they are signalling. Dolphins don't actually talk, they just squesal or honk. Also dolphins can not only communicate well but they can hear well too. They have there own natureal hearing system called Natural Sonor System. That means that they can hear and locate any objects in there path. So if a dolphin was in trouble 2 miles away another dolphin could understand where it is, by the dolphins signal and will go resue it. So you see dolphins are intelligent by there sences of hearing and communication.

Scientists have found that doplhins are the best known species of the water mammals. A dolphin is very intelligent, extremly nice, and very trainable. Many famous amusement parks, such as Seaworld, train dolphins to do about any trick or water stunt. Many tricks or water stunts include jumping out of the water and catching something like fish or jumping through a hoop. Most dolphins can jump to 20 ft. out of water. A dolphin will play with about anything too. So you see doplhins should be known as the best species of the water mammal from their intelligence. Now here is what there personality is like. I will let you decide if there friendly and nice. Also I think that dolphins are caring in a way because get this: A long time ago during World War II some men were stranded on a raft quite aways from shore. Two dolphins came up and pushed it to shore. Now I call that caring in a way. So the next time you are at a water amusement park with dophin, stop and watch. **(A computer was used to write this draft)**

Revision Defined

"As the author molds his work in revision, he continues to paint his picture with words..."

Revision is the third step in the writing process. The word "revision" means to re-see or see again with new eyes. This is why most authors put their drafts aside for at least a day before they start revising. It is a time to re-read and re-think your draft. The focus is on the content of your draft, not on spelling or punctuation. Your pre-write checklist will help you to reconsider your audience and purpose. Sharing your draft with others will tell you if your writing is clear and makes sense to your audience. The Reader R.A.P. Sheet in this chapter helps your reader to give you important information about your draft. You can share your draft with one or many readers: it's up to you.

When you fine tune your draft, you will decide what words, sentences and sections you want to add, delete or move to make your draft say exactly what you want it to. The R.A.D. Writer Sheet and Revision Symbols are in this chapter to guide you. You can cut and paste your changes or write them onto your draft. Many revisions are wonderfully messy. That's OK as long as you can still read everything.

Your draft is like an unpolished diamond. Revision is a magical, creative process in which your diamond begins to sparkle. *Have fun polishing!*

About This Chapter

This chapter includes...

A Revision Checklist

The **6 Step Revision Checklist** on page 50 is designed to guide you through the revision process. Each step is checked off after you complete it.

A R.A.D. Writer Sheet

The **R.A.D. Writer Sheet** on page 51 will help you decide what you want to **Re-place**, **Add** or **Delete**. Then you can use the **Revision Symbols** on the same page to make any changes.

A Reader R.A.P. Sheet

The **Reader R.A.P. Sheet** on page 53 will give your reader an opportunity to tell you what he liked about your draft and ask questions.

And Other Young Authors' Revisions

There are five revision examples in this chapter.

Revision Checklist Ingredients

The revision checklist helps a young author to easily follow the six basic steps of revision. He should keep this checklist with him during each step.

Materials:
Revision checklist (copy – page 113)
Your pre-writing checklist
Pencil/pen

Goal:
To check off each step of the revision process as you complete it

Steps:
1. Set aside your draft for at least 24 hours.
2. Read your draft aloud to a wall or a friend.
3. Look at your pre-write checklist and think about your audience and purpose. Does your draft stay true to them? Is it clear?
4. Fill out the R.A.D. Writer Sheet (see page 51).
5. Have a friend fill out the Reader R.A.P. Sheet (see page 53).

Revision Checklist Example

6 STEP REVISION CHECKLIST

 1. I took a writing break.

 2. I read my draft out loud.

 3. I thought about my audience and purpose.

 4. I used my R.A.D. Writer Sheet.

 5. My partner filled out the Reader R.A.P. Sheet for my draft.

 6. I made some changes.

Writer's Name: _Nick_

R.A.D. Writer Revision & Symbols

Some authors will cut and paste to re-place, add or delete sections in fine-tuning their drafts. The symbols below can be used to help standardize revision.

R.A.D. WRITER SHEET

Re-Place
- a word in a better spot
- a sentence in a better spot
- a paragraph in a better spot

Add
- any missing words
- any missing sentences
- more descriptive words

Delete
- repeated words
- words I don't need
- sentences I don't need

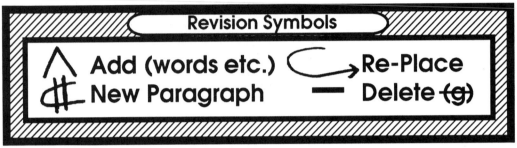

Revision Symbols

- ∧ Add (words etc.)
- ⌗ New Paragraph
- ↪ Re-Place
- — Delete ~~(g)~~

Materials:
R.A.D. Writer Sheet (copy – page 114)
6 Step Revision Checklist (copy – page 113)
Your draft
Pencil/pen

Goal:
To help you revise your draft

Steps:
1. Re-read your draft.
2. Ask yourself these questions:
   Does my draft make sense? Does it say what I want it to?
   What do I want to re-place, add or delete?
3. Refer to this sheet during revision.

Report Revision Example

Chapter 2 - Communication   Dolphins: Jessica

You know how dogs talk and they try to talk to ~~each~~ us? Well dolphins will do that too and other dolphins can under-stand what they are signalling. Dolphins don't actually talk, they just squesal or honk. Also dolphins can not only communicate well but they can hear well too. They have there own natureal hearing system called *a* Natural Sonor System. That means that they can hear and locate any objects in there path. So if a dolphin was in trouble *two* ~~2~~ miles away another dolphin could ~~understand~~ *would know* where it is, *through* ~~by~~ the dolphins signal and ~~will~~ *would* go resue it. So you see dolphins are intelli-gent ~~by~~ *through* there sences of hearing and communication.   **Chapter 1 - Intelligence**

Scientists ~~have found that~~ *know* doplhins ~~are the best known~~ *better than anyother* species of ~~the~~ water mammals. A dolphin is very intelligent, ex-tremly nice, and very ~~trainable~~ *easily trained*. Many famous amusement parks, such as Seaworld, train dolphins to do about any trick or water stunt. Many tricks or water stunts include jumping out of the water and catching something like fish or jumping through a hoop. Most dolphins can jump to 20 ft. out of *the* water. A dolphin will play with about anything too. So you see doplhins should be known as the best species of the water mammal for their intelligence. Now here is what there per-sonality is like. I will let you decide if there friendly and nice. Also I think that dolphins are caring in a way because get this: A long time ago during World War II some men were stranded on a raft quite ~~aways~~ *far* from shore. Two dolphins came up and pushed it to shore. Now I call that caring in a way. So the next time you are at a water amusement park with ~~dophin~~ *dolphins*, stop and watch.

Reader R.A.P. Revision

READER R.A.P.

Reader's Name Michelle
Writer's Name Steven

Read

  I read your writing

Ask

I'd like to know more about...
What is the witch's name?
Where does she go first?
How does the moon look?

Point out

I really liked...
I really liked your pictures
and the way your story
follows them. It reminds
me of a Halloween night.

One of the most valuable gifts an author can receive is constructive feedback about his writing. He wants to know if something is confusing and what his audience liked about his writing. It is an honor to be asked to view an author's piece. It should be done with great care and respect.

Materials:

Reader R.A.P. sheet (copy – page 114)
Your draft
Pencil/pen

Goals:

To help another author revise his draft
To read another author's writing
To tell the author the things you liked
To ask any questions

Steps:

1. Read the author's draft.
2. List things you want to know more about or which are confusing to you.
3. Write down the things you really liked.

Picture Story Revision Example

Hilda the ∧a Wich Gos up up ∧ in the ski a Wich She Sees the ∧ brit

moon and Wich Sees the Stre ∧butiful ∧O no and a Wich Hilda fullsdewn

Story Map Revision Example

Brandon   9/12/19

> 1 | First Place
>   Team

It was the day the day to sign up for baseball. I was really nervus. ∧ ~~I met~~ **Then my coach walked up to me**

~~my coch "hi Brandon"~~ and talked, ∧ ~~Well then~~ I had to get my uneform. ∧ ~~Whiel my~~ **for awhile. "Brandon called dad" on.**

~~dad helped me get in it~~ **I struggled to get in my uniform and my dad helped.** we had a praicte and we all did good. By now it

was time for our first game. ∧ **I was really excited.** We got there warmed up, then it was time to ~~PLAY~~ **PLAYBALL!**

~~BALL1~~ It started off pretty good we had ~~a~~ **an** eight run inning, they got 0. ∧ **on there's.** The

finel score was 15 to 5. By the ∧ ~~last game~~ **end of the season** our record was won-16 lost-2. We

were in the championships. It was time for the game. I was really nerves.

~~Finly~~ ∧ **It was an exciting game,** we won 5 to 4 we all got a first place trophy we ∧ ~~were realy~~ **all felt good and** happy.

The Eed

Four Square Revision Example

Nick
10-30-91 I went to Husky stadium, ^to see a football game with my friend ^Evan, my mom, and my dad, ^we When got ^We ate lots of peanuts and hot dogs. ~~went there~~, and I got a hat After the first half the huskies had 27 points. The Huskies won, and we ^by 57 to 0. ^and Evan got to went home on the bus. ^stay overnight.

Fast-writing Revision Example

Brigida

after a girl her mother read about in a book.

black and white skunk with a purple bow on one of her ears.   because it looked like a cave and she felt

red

Once there was a little ~~skunk~~/ Her name was Sari. One day she found a backpack. Sari climbed in. All

brave and ~~adventurous.~~

his

of a sudden it was dark! Someone picked up the backpack and put it on ~~their~~ back. Soon, Sari was asleep.

awoke

When she ~~woke up~~, she was in a closet! Luckily, the backpack was open. Sari climbed out and jumped on a

shelf. She was very hungry. But look! Over to the left were some small paper bags! Sari walked over to the

There were peanut butter sandwiches, oreo cookies, and chips too.

bags and climbed in one. Yum! The bag had delicious foods in it! Sari had a feast. ~~Sari decided to explore~~

the room outside of the closet. On dear! There are many children sitting at desks! Sari backed up. Suddenly,

It really scared her.

a bell rang! All of the children ran outside. What luck! Sari walked under the crackand climbed into an

open desk. Now there's one thing I should tell you. Never leave your desk opened or a skunk might climb

inside. Well, when Sari climbed inside the desk, the teacher said, "Oh Dear, Samantha left her desk opened!"

Then she closed her desk. Sari hid behind a watercolor set. When the children came in, they got ready to go

home. When Samantha opened her desk she found Sari. Sari ran out of the desk, into the hall and out to the

waving as they waited for her.

playground. There she found her pleasant family ~~waiting for her~~. Sari never went into a backpack again.

THE END

(This revision was cut and pasted together)

Chapter 5

Editing

Editing Defined

"In editing his masterpiece, he makes his work sparkle for his soon-to-be audience."

Editing is the fourth step in the writing process. Editing is very exciting because it is the last step before your final copy. It helps you to prepare your draft for publishing. In editing you will focus on the details in your writing. You will look for misspelled words, punctuation errors, and other grammatical mistakes.

Editing is like a game of hide and seek. The errors try to hide and you try to find them. It's fun to make a game of finding as many items to change as possible. Then give your draft to a friend and see if he can find anything else to change.

As you edit you will continue to polish your diamond. Soon you will share it with your audience. ***Have fun seeking!***

About This Chapter

This chapter includes...

An Editing Checklist

The **6 Step Editing Checklist** on page 62 is designed to guide you through the editing process. Each step is checked off after you complete it.

Editing Symbols

The **Editing Symbols** on page 63 will help you to make any changes to your text.

An Editor's Sheet

The **Editor's Sheet** on page 65 will give your reader an opportunity to help you find any items you might have missed in your own editing.

And Other Young Authors' Edited Drafts

There are five editing examples in this chapter.

Editing Checklist Ingredients

This checklist is designed to guide the writer through the editing process. The young author will determine when he feels his draft is edited to his satisfaction. For example, Steven (picture story-1st grader) decided his spelling was fine, but that he needed to add some punctuation marks.

Materials:
Editing checklist (copy – page 115)
Pencil/pen

Goal:
To go through the editing process

Steps:
1. Re-read your draft.
2. Check for any misspelled words.
3. Check to see if you capitalized the right words.
4. Have a partner check your draft using the Editor Sheet (see page 65).
5. Make your changes, checking off each box after you complete its editing step.

Editing Checklist Example

Editing Checklist

 1. I re-read my draft.

 2. I checked my spelling.

 3. I capitalized: the first word in a sentence
the names of people
the important title words

 4. I used punctuation marks:
at the end of a sentence (. ? !)
where needed in a sentence

 5. My partner checked my draft.
(using the editor sheet)

 6. I made some changes.

Writer's Name: _Nick_

Editing Symbols

My Editing Symbols

Symbol	Meaning	Example
sp	The word is spelled incorrectly.	I saw a gost on Howl- sp oween. sp
≡	Change a small letter to a capital letter.	I went to the party with mary.
/	Change a capital letter to a small letter.	I stopped to get the Mail.
e	Remove punctuation, words or sentences.	The fair was exciting e And it was fun.
#	Start new paragraph.	# I like to eat apple pie.
→	Indent the sentence.	→ Our team won. They ...

Story Map Editing Example

Brandon   9/12/(19)

1 | First Place
  | Team

→

It was the day to sign up for baseball. I was really nervus [*nervous* sp]. Then my coach walked

up to me and talked for awhile. I called "dad" because I had to get my uneform [*uniform* sp]

on. I struggled to get in my uniform and my dad helped. We had our first praicte [*practice* sp]

and we all did very good. (Chapter 2) By now it was time for our first game. I was really ex-

cited. We got there, warmed up, then it was time to PLAYBALL! It started off

pretty good we had an eight run inning, they got 0 on theres [*theirs* sp]. The finel [*final* sp] score was (Chapter 3)

15 to 5. By the end of the season our record was won-16. lost-2. We were in the

championships. It was time for the game. I was really nerves [*nervous* sp]. It was an exciting

game we won 5 to 4 and we all got a first place trophy we all felt good and realy [*really* sp]

happy.

End

The Eed [sp]

Editor's Sheet

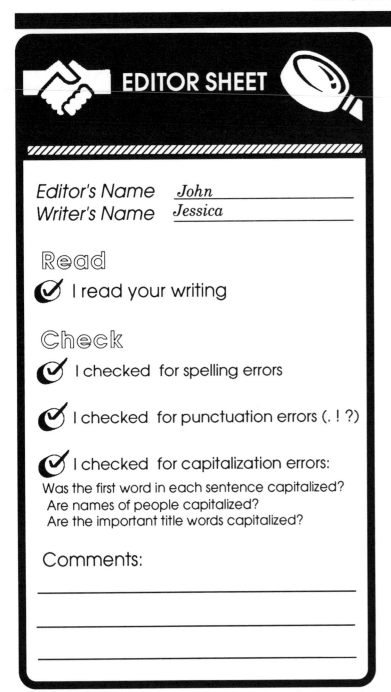

Editor's Name   *John*
Writer's Name   *Jessica*

Read
☑ I read your writing

Check
☑ I checked for spelling errors

☑ I checked for punctuation errors (. ! ?)

☑ I checked for capitalization errors:
Was the first word in each sentence capitalized?
Are names of people capitalized?
Are the important title words capitalized?

Comments:
_____
_____
_____

It is very helpful to have young authors buddy up and cross check each other's writing.

Materials:
Editor sheet (copy – page 115)
Your draft
Pencil/pen

Goal:
To help another author edit his draft

Steps:
1. Read the author's draft.
2. Check for spelling errors.
3. Check for punctuation errors.
4. Check for capitalization errors.
5. After you have completed each step, place a checkmark in its circle.

Report Editing Example

Dolphins: Jessica

Chapter 1: Intelligence

Scientists know dolphins better than any other species of water mammals. A dolphin is very intelligent, extremely nice, and very easily trained. Many famous amusement parks, such as Seaworld, train dolphins to do about any trick or water stunt. Many tricks or water stunts include jumping out of the water and catching something like fish or jumping through a hoop. Most dolphins can jump to 20 ft. out of the water. A dolphin will play with about anything too. So you see doplhins ~~dolphins~~ SP should be known as the best species of the water mammal for their intelligence.

Now here is what there ~~their~~ SP personality is like. I will let you decide if there ~~they're~~ SP friendly and nice. Also, I think that dolphins are caring in a way because get this: A long time ago during World War II some men were stranded on a raft quite far from shore. Two dolphins came and pushed them to shore. Now I call that caring in a way. So the next time you are at a water amusement park with a dophin, stop and watch.

Chapter 2 - Communication

You know how dogs talk and they try to talk to us? Well dolphins will do that too and other dolphins can understand what they are signalling. Dolphins don't actually talk, they just sqesal ~~squeal~~ SP or honk. Also dolphins can not only communicate well but they can hear well too. They have there ~~their~~ own natureal ~~natural~~ SP hearing system called a Natural Sonor System. That means that they can hear and locate any objects in there ~~their~~ SP path. So if a dolphin was in trouble two miles away, another dolphin would know where it is, through the dolphins signal and would go resue it. So you see dolphins are intelligent through there senses ~~their senses~~ SP SP of hearing and communication.

Four Square Editing Example

Nick

I went to Husky stadiam ^{sp} to see a football game with evan, my mom, and my dad.

When we got there I got a hat. We ate lots of peanuts and hot dogs. After the first half the huskies had 27 points. The Huskies won by 57 to 0. we went home on the bus, and Evan got to stay overnight.

Picture Story Editing Example

Hilda the Wich Gos up in the ski. She sees the brit

moon and sees the butiful stre. O no! Hilda fulls dewn

Chapter 6

Publishing

Publishing Defined

"Then he proudly presents his special, published, one-of-a-kind creation in book form."

Publishing is the fifth and final step in the writing process. In publishing your book you re-write your revised and edited draft into its final form. You prepare your book for its audience. You decide the type of book you want it to be.

Published books have special pages inside. You will create a title page, and you may want to dedicate your book to someone on a dedication page. Your reader will also want to know something about you. It makes reading a book even more interesting when you learn about its author, so you will prepare an "about the author" page. Many young authors include a comments page at the back of the book for readers to tell what they liked best. Some chapter books and reports include a table of contents and a bibliography (see page 80).

In this chapter you will find examples of all the special publishing pages and book types. Chapter 7 will give directions on how to make the six different types of books shown.

Publishing your book is a wonderfully creative experience. Soon you will share your special book with its audience. It is a time to be very proud of yourself. ***Have fun sharing your creation!***

About This Chapter

This chapter includes...

A Publishing Checklist

The **Publishing Checklist** on page 73 is designed to guide you through the publishing process. It includes information about the special pages found in a published book.

And Young Author Publishing Examples

There are examples of book covers, title pages, dedication pages, inside pages, about the author pages, a bibliography, a table of contents and a comments page.

Publishing Checklist

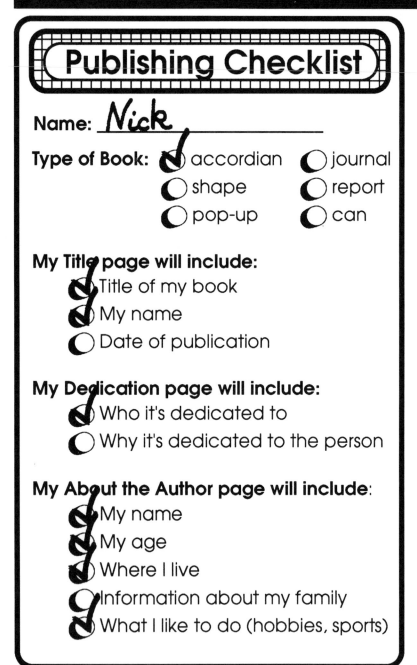

Name: Nick

Type of Book:
- ☑ accordian
- ○ shape
- ○ pop-up
- ○ journal
- ○ report
- ○ can

My Title page will include:
- ☑ Title of my book
- ☑ My name
- ○ Date of publication

My Dedication page will include:
- ☑ Who it's dedicated to
- ○ Why it's dedicated to the person

My About the Author page will include:
- ☑ My name
- ☑ My age
- ☑ Where I live
- ○ Information about my family
- ☑ What I like to do (hobbies, sports)

Materials:
Publishing checklist (copy – page 116)
Your revised and edited draft
Pencil/pen/marker

Goal:
To help you make publishing choices

Steps:
1. Choose the type of book you want to make.
2. Check the things you want to include in each publishing page.

Book Cover Examples

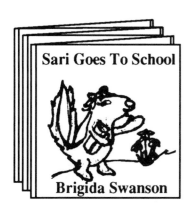

Brigida's Accordian Book

Steven's Pop-Up Book

Brandon's Can Book

Terry's Journal

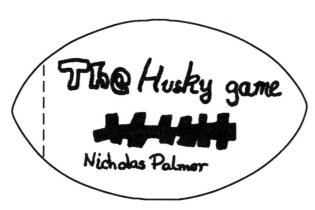

Nick's Shape Book

Jessica's Report

Title Page Examples

Sari Goes to School

by

Brigida Swanson
10/91

Brigida's Accordian Book

Hilda the Wich

Steven Yoo

12/05/91

Steven's Pop-Up Book

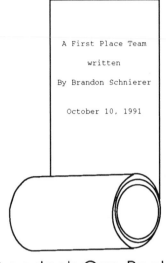

A First Place Team

written

By Brandon Schnierer

October 10, 1991

Brandon's Can Book

My Journal
by
Terry Yoo

Terry's Journal

The Husky game
by Nick Palmer

Nick's Shape Book

Dolphins
By: Jessica Ruble

Jessica's Report

Dedication Page Examples

This book is dedicated to my sister Juleah

Brigida's Accordian Book

This book is dedicated to

my mom

Steven's Pop-Up Book

Dedicated to My Baseball Team

Brandon's Can Book

this book is dedicated to

my teacher

Terry's Journal

Dedicated to My mom and dad

Nick's Shape Book

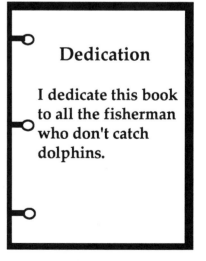

Dedication

I dedicate this book to all the fisherman who don't catch dolphins.

Jessica's Report

Inside Page Examples

It was the day, the day to sign up for baseball. I was really nervous then my coach walked up to me and we stood and talked for a while.

Once there was a little black and white skunk with a purple bow on one of her ears. Her name was Sari, after a girl her mother read about in a book.
1.

One day she found a red back pack. Sari climbed in because it looked like a cave and she felt brave and adventurous. All of a sudden it was dark!
2.

Brigida's Accordian Book

Brandon's Can Book

Steven's Pop-Up Book

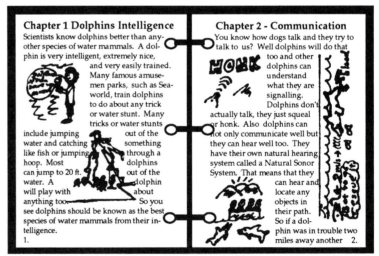

Chapter 1 Dolphins Intelligence
Scientists know dolphins better than any-other species of water mammals. A dol-phin is very intelligent, extremely nice, and very easily trained. Many famous amuse-men parks, such as Sea-world, train dolphins to do about any trick or water stunt. Many tricks or water stunts include jumping out of the water and catching something like fish or jumping through a hoop. Most dolphins can jump to 20 ft. out of the water. A dolphin will play with about anything too. So you see dolphins should be known as the best species of water mammals from their in-telligence.
1.

Chapter 2 - Communication
You know how dogs talk and they try to talk to us? Well dolphins will do that too and other dolphins can understand what they are signalling. Dolphins don't actually talk, they just squeal or honk. Also dolphins can not only communicate well but they can hear well too. They have their own natural hearing system called a Natural Sonor System. That means that they can hear and locate any objects in their path. So if a dol-phin was in trouble two miles away another 2.

HONK

Jessica's Report

About the Author Page Examples

About the Author

My name is Brigida Swanson, I am 11 years old. I live in Bellevue,WA. I have a 9 year old sister named Juleah and a cat named Cuddles. I like to play soccer and draw and I like animals.

7.

Brigida's Accordian Book

My name is Steven. I am 6½ years old. I live in Redmond WA. I go to School at Redmond El. I like to play Soccer. My twin brother is Terry

Steven's Pop-Up Book

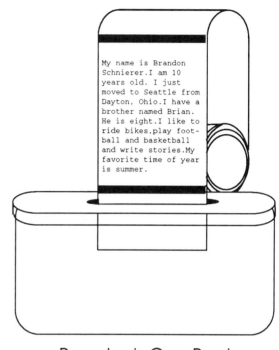

My name is Brandon Schnierer.I am 10 years old. I just moved to Seattle from Dayton, Ohio.I have a brother named Brian. He is eight.I like to ride bikes,play foot-ball and basketball and write stories.My favorite time of year is summer.

Brandon's Can Book

About the Author

My name is Terry. I am 6½ years old. I was born in California. I am a Korean-American. I like to play Nintendo. My favrit food is pizza I live in Tuscany.

Terry's Journal

My name is Nick Palmer. I am 7¾ years old. I live in Woodinville,Wa. My favorite books are the Box Car Children. I like to play Nintendo.

Nick's Shape Book

About the Author
Jessica is in 5th grade. She has three sisters and 1 brother. She is the middle child. Bummer!

Jessica likes to dance, draw, swim, write stories and go shopping. She hates homework.

Her hometown is Los Altos, California.   9.

Jessica's Report

Examples of Other Kinds of Pages

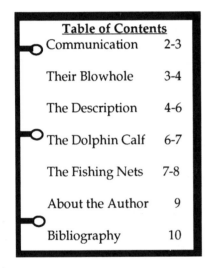

Jessica's Table of Contents

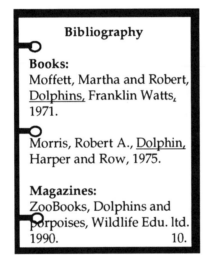

Jessica's Bibliography

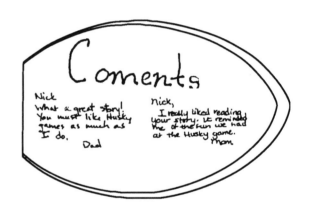

Nick's Comments Page

Chapter 7
Books To Make

Books You Can Make

"He has painted a picture with words. He has sculpted his story on paper. He is a creative and truly talented young author: a sight for all to behold!"

When you make your book - you get to decide what style will be just right for your writing. You might choose to make an accordian book to display your whole story at once or maybe a pop-up book so your illustrations will pop right out at your audience.

This chapter shows you how to make the six different book styles that the <u>Book-Write</u> young authors chose to house their writing. The directions can be changed to create an even more personal and unique book for you. Try making a shoe box book instead of a can book or a cloth journal instead of a wallpapered journal. There are also some recycling ideas for you to try. Whenever possible, re-use household items as book parts.

Use your imagination as you create a special book cover to house your very special diamond.

Bookmaking Material Information

Cans

The can book works very well with an oblong gourmet coffee can because adding machine paper is exactly the right size for the can. However, you can make this book with any can that has a plastic lid. Just use white paper for the cover instead of adding machine paper.

Cardboard

Cardboard can be found in the packaging of many household and personal products. Depending on the thickness, it can be difficult to cut or fold. However, thin cardboard pieces used to package pantyhose and shirts are just the right thickness for book covers. An older author may also enjoy taking cereal boxes apart and using them for cardboard.

Railroad board

If you want a thicker (4 ply) material that comes in many different colors, check into railroad board. It costs approximately $1.00 for a 22" X 28" sheet.

Recycled or Re-used paper

Whenever you can, try to use recycled paper. If you don't have recycled paper, save the unused backs of paper and re-use them for pages you paste onto other book materials. Make sure the existing writing doesn' t show through first.

Tagboard

Tagboard is a wonderful material. You can usually find it at art supply stores. It is inexpensive (about 80¢ per sheet), easy to cut and easy to fold. It comes in manilla or white 24" X 36" sheets. It is great for all types of covers.

Making a Shape Book

Shape books are easy to make and young authors love them. Try making lots of different shapes based on the theme of the story.

Materials:
- Construction paper
- Glue stick/paste
- Paper
- Scissors
- Pen/pencil/markers

Steps:
1. Decide upon the shape of your book and trace it onto the construction paper.
2. Fold the paper in half and cut two covers.
3. Cut out the number of pages you want inside the cover. Write your story onto the pages. Staple the pages to the back cover and cut the front cover shape in half.
4. Staple the two front covers onto the back cover so that it opens from the middle.
5. Fold back the front covers to crease it open.

Recycling Ideas:
1. Use cereal box cardboard for cover shapes.
2. Glue pictures from magazines to create the cover design you want.

Shape Book Directions

Step 1

Trace the shape of your book onto construction paper.

Step 2

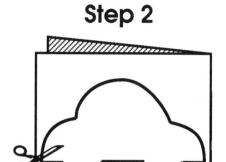

Fold paper in half and cut two covers.

Step 3

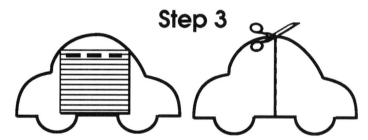

Cut book pages to fit inside the cover. Write story on pages. Staple pages to back cover. Cut front cover shape in half.

Step 4

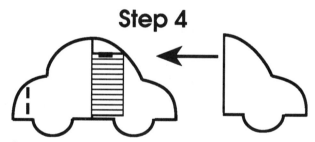

Staple front covers onto the back cover.

Step 5

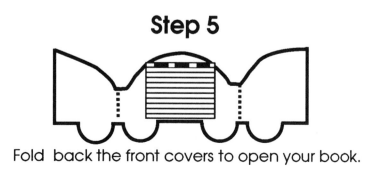

Fold back the front covers to open your book.

Shape Book

Making an Accordian Book

An accordian book works well for short stories and poems. When made out of tagboard it stands up by itself and is a wonderful way to display a young author's work. It can also be made out of many other materials.

Materials:
- Tagboard
- Glue stick/paste
- Paper
- Scissors
- Pen/pencil/markers

Steps:
1. Decide upon the shape of your book and trace your shape onto the tagboard.
2. Determine the number of pages in your book and cut them out of the tagboard.
3. Tape the book pages together on the front side, then turn them over and tape the back.
4. Cut sheets of paper to fit inside the pages. Write your story and draw the illustrations on the paper. Glue your finished story onto the tagboard.

Recycling Ideas:
1. Use cardboard from inside a pantyhose box.
2. Write on the clean side of used paper.

Accordian Book Directions

Step 1

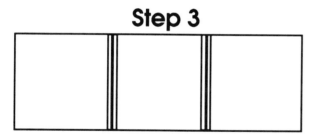

Trace your shape onto the tagboard.

Step 2

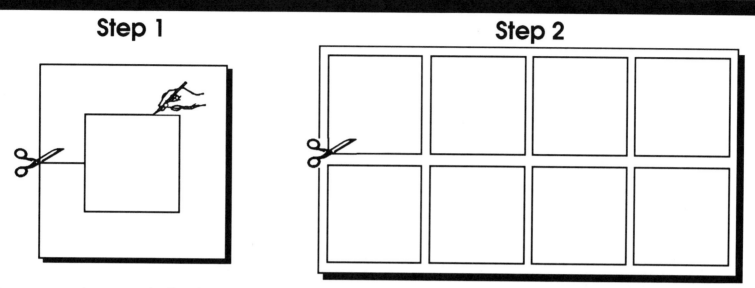

Cut out your book pieces. (2 for cover + 1 for each page)

Step 3

Tape pieces together front and back on both sides of the tagboard.

Step 4

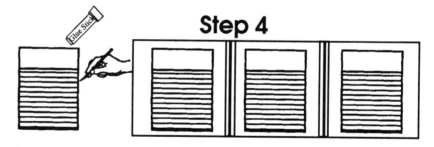

Cut sheets of paper to fit your book pieces. Write your story, draw illustrations and glue sheets onto the page.

Accordian Book

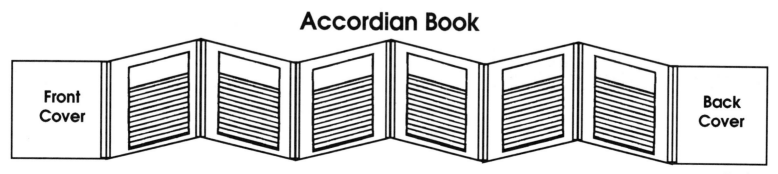

Front Cover

Back Cover

Making a Can Book

Can books are really fun to make and read. They promote recycling by re-using a household item. Younger authors will need assistance in making this book.*

Materials:
- Empty oblong can like a gourmet coffee can
- Scissors*
- Pen/pencil/markers
- Glue stick/paste
- Adding machine tape

Steps:
1. Take your can and wrap adding machine paper around it until it just overlaps. Then cut the paper.
2. Measure your can front and mark it in pencil. Draw your cover between your marks.
3. Glue the cover onto your can.
4. Cut an opening into the plastic lid just a bit longer than the width of your paper and wide enough to let the paper slip through easily.*
5. Write directly onto the adding machine paper. (Some authors paste on typed text)
6. Roll up your story and pull it through the lid.

Can Book Directions

Step 1

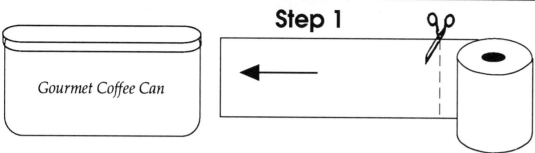

Wrap adding machine paper around can until it overlaps. Cut paper.

Step 2

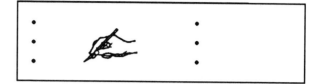

Measure front of can, mark paper and draw cover on this section.

Step 3

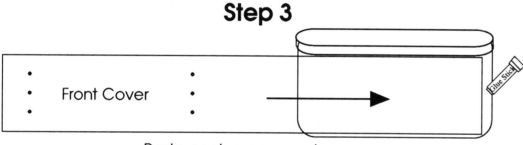

Paste or glue cover onto can.

Step 4

Cut opening into can lid.

Step 5

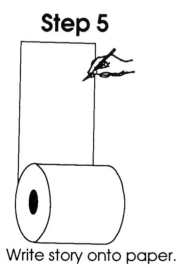

Write story onto paper.

Step 6

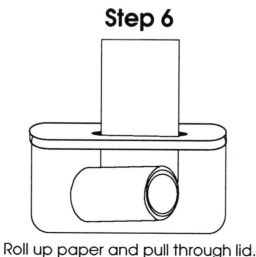

Roll up paper and pull through lid.

Can Book

Making a Pop-Up Book

Young authors may need some assistance in making their first pop-up book. Pop-up books should be used with shorter stories as it is difficult to bind too many pages together. It is a very fun book to read.

Materials:

- Construction Paper
- Glue stick/paste
- White paper
- Scissors
- Pen/pencil/markers

Steps:

1. Cut your construction paper cover and white pages in a rectangular shape.
2. Fold your cover in half, forming a front and back cover. Draw your cover, then set it aside.
3. Fold your first page in half. Mark two lines in the center about one inch apart and one inch down. Cut on the lines.
4. Open the page and fold the cut piece inside.
5. Draw the pop-up shapes for each page.
6. Cut out each shape.
7. Glue shape to the front of pop-out section.
8. Flatten the page out and write your story.
9. Complete all pages. Glue the back side of one page to the front side of the next.
10. Glue your cover to the book pages.

Pop-Up Book Directions

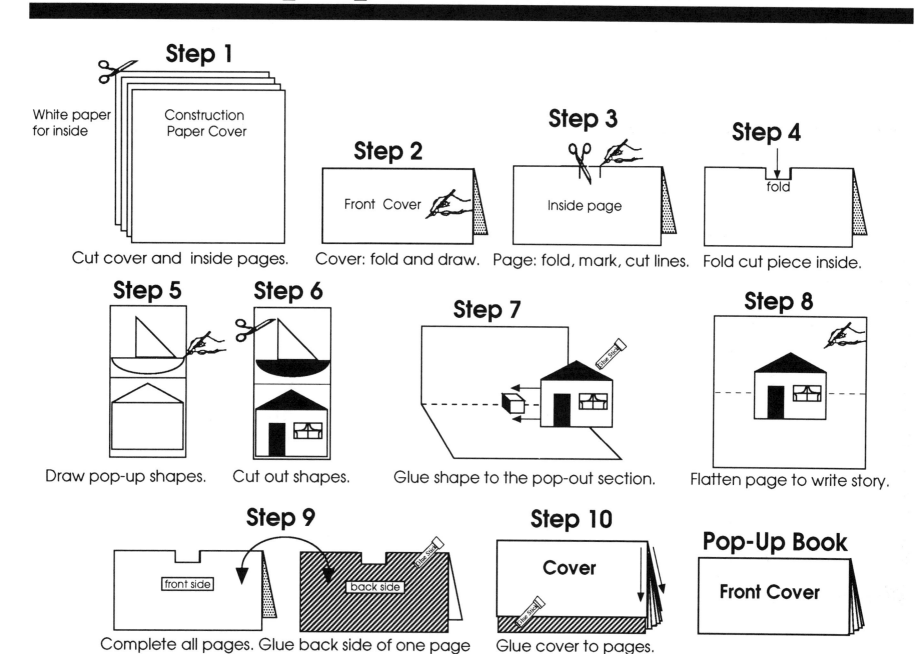

Step 1

White paper for inside

Construction Paper Cover

Cut cover and inside pages.

Step 2

Front Cover

Cover: fold and draw.

Step 3

Inside page

Page: fold, mark, cut lines.

Step 4

fold

Fold cut piece inside.

Step 5

Draw pop-up shapes.

Step 6

Cut out shapes.

Step 7

Glue Stick

Glue shape to the pop-out section.

Step 8

Flatten page to write story.

Step 9

front side

Glue Stick

back side

Complete all pages. Glue back side of one page to front side of next page.

Step 10

Cover

Glue Stick

Glue cover to pages.

Pop-Up Book

Front Cover

Making a Journal

Journals are very personal. They can also be made with cloth remnants or leftover contact paper.

Materials:
- Cardboard
- Glue stick/paste
- Paper
- Wallpaper
- Scissors
- Pen/pencil/markers
- Stapler

Steps:
1. Trace your book shape and cut two covers.
2. Trace a 1" border around the covers on back side of the wallpaper. Make a 90° cut on each corner.
3. Glue your cardboard cover to the backside of the wallpaper. Glue each wallpaper edge and fold it on top of the cardboard.
4. Cut and glue a smaller piece of wallpaper to the inside cover.
5. Determine the number of pages you want in your book and cut them to fit inside.
6. Put your pages inside the two covers.
7. Staple the whole book together.
8. Cut a small wallpaper piece and glue it to the spine of your journal.

Journal Directions

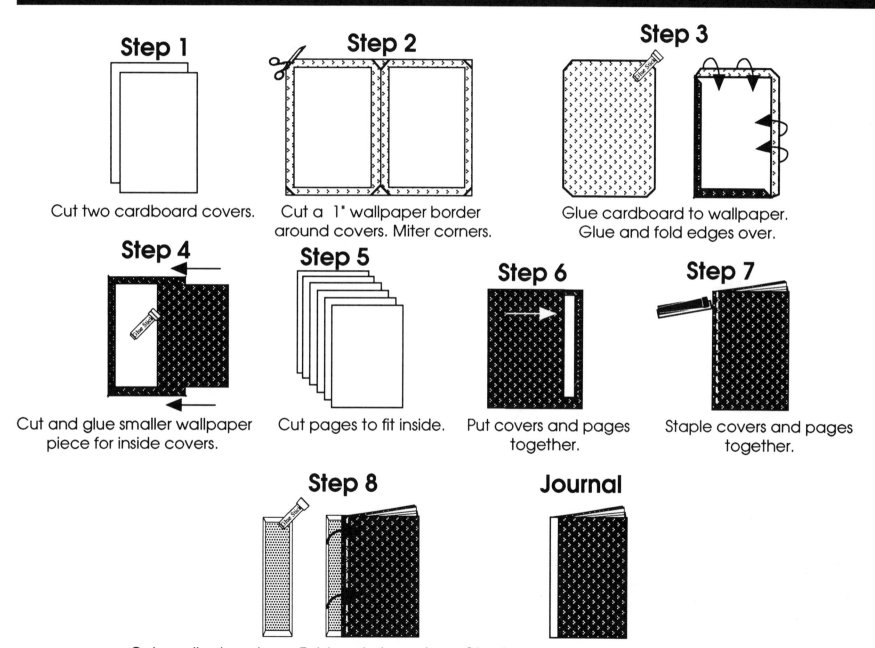

Step 1

Cut two cardboard covers.

Step 2

Cut a 1" wallpaper border around covers. Miter corners.

Step 3

Glue cardboard to wallpaper. Glue and fold edges over.

Step 4

Cut and glue smaller wallpaper piece for inside covers.

Step 5

Cut pages to fit inside.

Step 6

Put covers and pages together.

Step 7

Staple covers and pages together.

Step 8

Cut small spine piece. Fold and glue edges. Glue to covers.

Journal

Making a Report

Reports can be made out of all types of materials.

Materials:
- Poster board
- Hole punch
- Paper
- Scissors
- Pen/pencil/markers
- Yarn

Steps:
1. Cut the front and back covers out of poster board.
2. Punch holes into the two covers.
3. Draw your cover onto the poster board or paste on your prepared items.
4. Write or type your story onto letter sized paper.
5. Place the finished pages inside the covers.
6. Use yarn to tie the covers and pages together.

Recycling Ideas:
1. Write your report on recycled paper.
2. Re-shape styrofoam package inserts for a three dimensional report cover.

Report Directions

Step 1

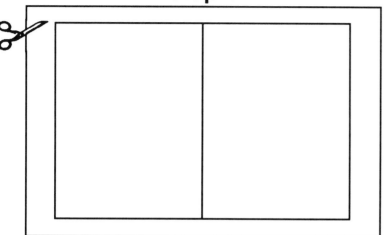

Cut two covers out of colored poster board.

Step 2

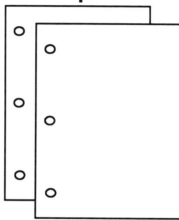

Punch holes into covers.

Step 3

Draw cover or paste on prepared items.

Step 4

Write or type your story on letter sized paper.

Step 5

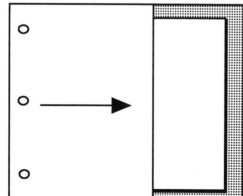

Place completed pages inside covers.

Report

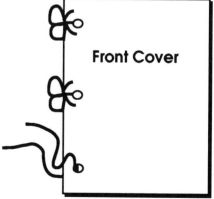

Front Cover

Use yarn to tie covers and pages together.

Chapter 8

Glossary

Glossary

Accordian Book

A book that folds open like an accordian.

Audience

The people who read your book.

Author

A person who tells a story with words or pictures.

Brainstorming

A technique used to help an author think of things to write about.

Biography

Writing about a person's life.

Can Book

A book made out of a can.

Challenge

To make something more exciting. Trying something new that will use what you already know and also teach you new things.

Conclusion

The ending of a story.

Create

To take an idea and make something out of it. This book is written to help you create your own books.

Dedicate

To honor a person who is special to you by writing in their name on your dedication page. To show your appreciation.

Delete

To erase or cross something out.

Description

Using words to explain what something is like. To give someone information about something.

Determine

To decide what you want to do. To make up your mind.

Draft

An unfinished piece of writing. The second step in the writing process.

Edit

A time when you check your writing for any changes you want to make in spelling and punctuation.

Editor

The person you ask to help you find possible spelling and punctuation changes.

Glossary

Example
Showing how something was done by someone else.

Fairy Tale
A make-believe story about imaginary creatures.

Grammar
Rules for how words should be put together.

Illustrate
To draw a picture.

Journal
A book you write into regularly.

Main Character
The main person in a story. The person in the story more than anyone else.

Map out
To plan something out in detail.

Organize
To put something together in a logical and orderly way.

Perspective
The way you see a situation. The way someone sees something or views it.

Plot
How a story will unfold. The things that will happen in your story.

Pop-Up Book
A book that has at least one illustration that pops out when you open it up.

Process
To do or make something through special steps.

Punctuation
The marks used in writing (like .,!:;). Punctuation marks help make writing easier to understand.

Reconsider
To think about something again.

Recycle
To use an item again instead of throwing it away. Recycling helps save our natural resources.

Report
To give information about a topic in a logical way.

Glossary

Re-place

To place a word or sentence in another spot.

Research

To find information about a topic. To study something carefully.

Revision

To see again with new eyes. To check your writing to make sure it says what you want it to.

Setting

The location and time period in which your story takes place.

Shape Book

A book that is made in a special shape.

Spin off

When an idea comes from another idea.

Technique

A tool used to help someone do something.

Unique

One of a kind. Not like any other.

Chapter 9

Resources

Places That Publish Young Authors' Writing

Magazine and Address	Age Level	What They Like to Publish
Children's Album P.O. Box 6086 Concord, CA 94524	8 to 14	Stories, plays, artwork, poems (less than 50 lines) and book reviews *Notes:* Reviews should include the author's name, book title, publisher, number of pages, what the book is about, what you learned, if it was fun to read and why you think other kids your age would like to read it. Artwork should be in full color and no less than 8" x 10".
Child Life **Children's Digest** **Children's Playmate** **Jack and Jill** Children's Health Institute 1100 Waterway Blvd. P.O. Box 567 Indianapolis, IN 46206	8 to 12 (pre-teens) 6 to 8 7 to 10	Stories, poetry, jokes, riddles, and occasional art Stories, poetry, jokes, and riddles Poetry, drawings, jokes, and riddles Jokes, riddles, stories, poetry, and drawings
Creative Kids P.O. Box 6086 Concord, CA 94524	8 to 14	Poetry, music, puzzles, activites, parodies, limericks, plays, cartoons, artwork, photography, book reviews and games *Notes:* All submissions must have your name, birthdate, home address, school name and school address. A self-addressed, stamped envelope is required.

Places That Publish Young Authors' Writing

Magazine and Address	Age level	What They Like to Publish
Cricket Open Court Publishing Co. 1058 Eight Street LaSalle, Ill 61301	13 and under	*Notes:* They sponsor poetry and art contests every month. The contest winners are published. You have to read the magazine to know the contest rules. You might find it at your library.
The McGuffey Writer The McGuffey Foundation School 5128 Westgate Drive Oxford, OH 45056 (All children's writing)	K-6th	Short stories, essays, poetry, cartoons, and black and white artwork *Notes:* Each page must be submitted with your name, grade level, school, address and signed by a teacher or parent.
STONE SOUP: the magazine for children P.O. Box 83 Santa Cruz, CA 95063 (All children's writing)	13 and under	Stories, poems, book reviews and art *Notes:* They prefer writing and art based on personal experience. Send samples of your artwork. If you want to review books, write and tell them about yourself. Enclose a self-addressed, stamped envelope with writing or artwork.

Book Publisher

Landmark Editions, Inc. P.O. Box 4469 1420 Kansas Ave. Kansas City, MO 64127		*Notes:* Landmark is a company that publishes books written by young authors. To enter this contest you must write for their rules and guidelines sheet. Look for their books in your library.

Other Bookmaking Resources

Author	Book Title	Publisher
Atwell, Nancie	*In the Middle*	Heinemann Educational Books, 1987
Calkins, Lucy McCormick	*The Art of Teaching Writing*	Heinemann Educational Books, 1986
Calkins, Lucy McCormick	*Lessons from a Child*	Heinemann Educational Books, 1983
Evans, Joy Moore, Jo Ellen	*How to Make Books with Children*	Evan-Moore Corporation, 1983
Evans, Joy Moore, Jo Ellen	*How to Make Books with Children-Volume 2*	Evan-Moore Corporation, 1991
Freed, Judith	*Freed's Guide to Student Competitions and Publishing**	Fountainpen Press, 1991
Graves, Donald H.	*Writing: Teachers and Children at Work*	Heinemann Educational Books, 1983
Graves, Donald H. Stuart, Virginia	*Write From the Start*	Plume, New American Library, 1986

*To order Freed's Guide to Student Competitions and Publishing, *write to Fountainpen Press, 218 West Fountain Ave., Delaware, Ohio 43015. This book has 120 contests for students K-12.*

Chapter 10

Forms To Copy

Pre-Writing Checklist

Pre-Writing Checklist

Purpose

Why...
do you want to write your book?

- ◐ I want to tell a story
- ◐ I 'm writing a report
- ◐ Just for fun
- ◐ Write your own reason:

Audience

Who...
do you want to read your book?

- ◐ Friend
- ◐ Parent
- ◐ Grandparent
- ◐ Brother
- ◐ Sister
- ◐ Teacher
- ◐ Librarian
- ◐ Others:

Pre-Writing Technique

Which...
technique would you like to use?

to determine your topic...

- ◐ Brainstorming
- ◐ Idea List

to think before you write...

- ◐ Picture Story
- ◐ Four Square W's
- ◐ Story Map
- ◐ Idea Chart
- ◐ Report
- ◐ Other:

Topic

What...
topic did you decide upon?
(Write in after you've finished pre-writing)

_____

My Name is: Date:

Forms from <u>Book-Write</u>, a MicNik Publication.

Idea List

Things I want to write about

	Pre-Write	Draft	Revision	Edit	Publish

Brainstorming

Name: _____

IDEAS

Forms from <u>Book-Write</u>, a MicNik Publication.

Four Square W's Pre-Write

Name:_____

Topic

[   ]

Who? Where?

What happens first?

What happens next?

What is the ending?

Idea Chart Pre-Write

Name: _____

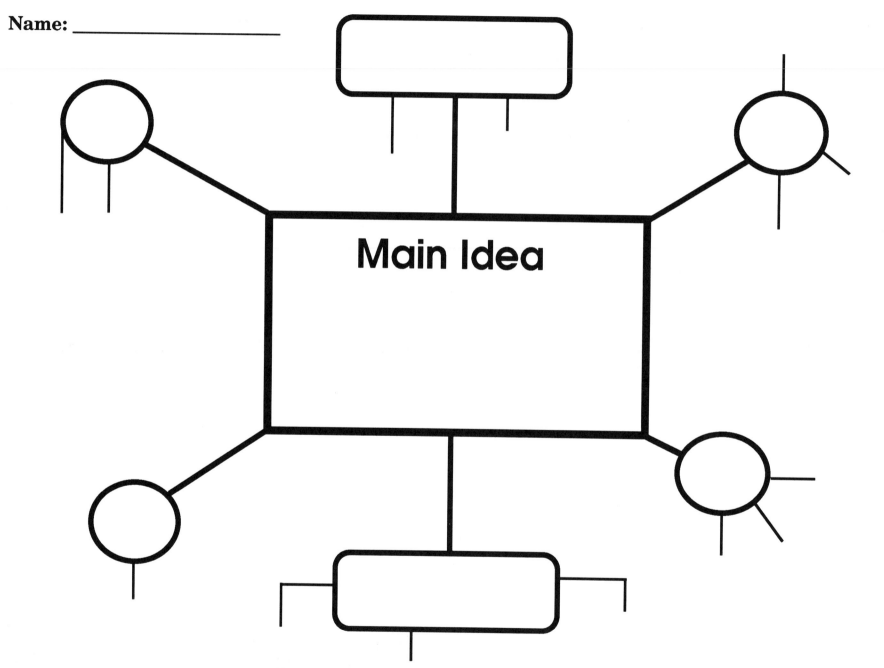

Main Idea

Forms from <u>Book-Write</u>, a MicNik Publication.

Story Map Pre-Write

Name: _____

Story Topic: _____

Main Character(s)

Supporting Characters

Supporting Characters

Setting

Plot

Conclusion

Forms from <u>Book-Write</u>, a MicNik Publication.

Report Flow-Chart Pre-Write

Name: _____

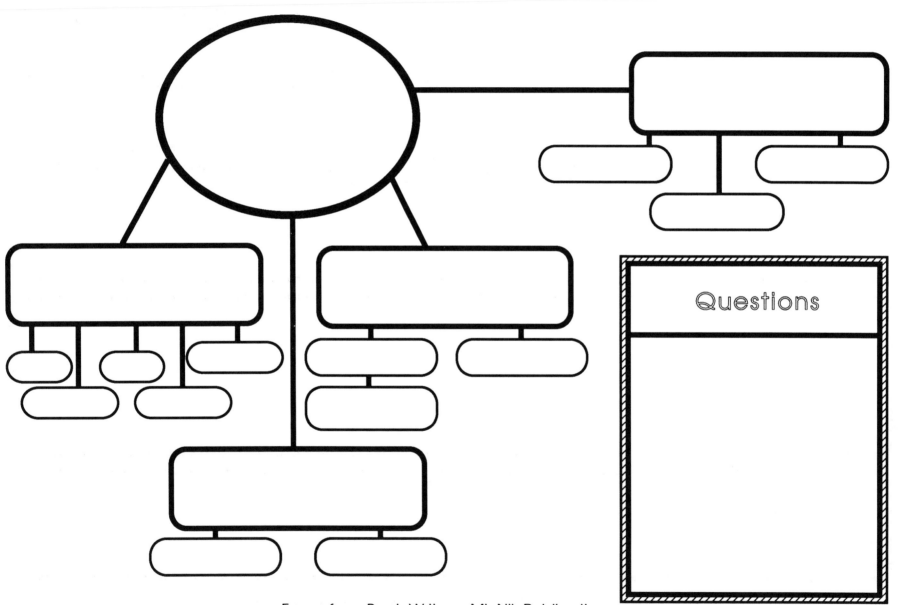

Forms from <u>Book-Write</u>, a MicNik Publication.

Draft Checklist

Draft Checklist

Name_____

1. My topic from Pre-writing is

_____

2. My audience is

_____

My form of writing will be...

○ short story   ○ poetry
○ journal writing   ○ play
○ report   ○ biography
○ fairy tale

My writing voice will be...

○ myself   ○ an alien
○ a story character   ○ an object
○ a famous person   ○ my teacher
○ one of my parents   ○ a pet
○ a person in the future ○ other:

Revision Checklist

☐ 1. I took a writing break.

☐ 2. I read my draft out loud.

☐ 3. I thought about my audience and purpose.

☐ 4. I used my R.A.D. Writer Sheet.

☐ 5. My partner filled out the Reader R.A.P. Sheet for my draft.

☐ 6. I made some changes.

Writer's Name:_____

Forms from Book-Write, a MicNik Publication.

Revision Sheets

R.A.D. WRITER SHEET ✂

Name: _____

Re-Place

○ a word in a better spot

○ a sentence in a better spot

○ a paragraph in a better spot

Add

○ any missing words

○ any missing sentences

○ more descriptive words

Delete

○ repeated words

○ words I don't need

○ sentences I don't need

READER R.A.P. SHEET

Reader's Name _____

Writer's Name _____

Read

○ I read your writing

Ask

I'd like to know more about...

_____
_____
_____
_____

Point out

I really liked...

_____
_____
_____
_____

Forms from <u>Book-Write</u>, a MicNik Publication.

Editing Sheets

Editing Checklist

☐ 1. I re-read my draft.

☐ 2. I checked my spelling.

☐ 3. I capitalized: the first word in a sentence
the names of people
the important title words

☐ 4. I used punctuation marks:
at the end of a sentence (. ? !)
where needed in a sentence

☐ 5. My partner checked my draft.
(using the editor sheet)

☐ 6. I made some changes.

Writer's Name:_____

EDITOR SHEET

Editor's Name _____
Writer's Name _____

Read

○ I read your writing

Check

○ I checked for spelling errors

○ I checked for punctuation errors (. ! ?)

○ I checked for capitalization errors:
Was the first word in each sentence capitalized?
Are names of people capitalized?
Are the important title words capitalized?

Comments:

_____

_____

_____

Forms from Book-Write, a MicNik Publication.

Publishing Checklist

Publishing Checklist

Name: _____

Type of Book:
- ○ accordian
- ○ shape
- ○ pop-up
- ○ journal
- ○ report
- ○ can

My Title page will include:
- ○ Title of my book
- ○ My name
- ○ Date of publication

My Dedication page will include:
- ○ Who it's dedicated to
- ○ Why it's dedicated to the person

My About the Author Page will include:
- ○ My name
- ○ My age
- ○ Where I live
- ○ Information about my family
- ○ What I like to do (hobbies, sports)

Forms from Book-Write, a MicNik Publication.

ABOUT THE AUTHOR

Michelle received her undergraduate and graduate degrees at the University of Washington. She is an educational consultant and author. Michelle is 37 years old and lives in the Pacific Northwest with her son and husband. She loves writing and working with young authors and readers. She writes music and enjoys singing with children.

Her first book, *Through My Eyes*, was co-authored with her son, Nicholas, when he was five years old and illustrated by the children in his kindergarten class. Her latest book, *Book-Talk*, encourages a lifelong love of literature through fun, exciting reading experiences and projects. Michelle always includes childrens' work in her books.

MicNik Publications

Book-Talk does for reading what *Book-Write* does for writing. It is a fun, clear, easy-to-follow resource guide for teachers and parents who want to encourage a lifelong love of literature. *Book-Talk* is filled with real kids' examples and reproducible forms.

11" x 81/2" • 160 pages • $16.95
ISBN 1-879235-02-1
(WA State tax – $1.45)

A fun, easy-to-follow, bookmaking guide for young authors. Filled with examples of other young authors' books. A wonderful resource for teachers and parents interested in the writing process. Reproducible forms for use in the classroom or at home.

11" x 81/2" • 128 pages • $16.95
ISBN 1-879235-01-3
(WA State tax – $1.45)

A look at life through the eyes of a young child. Co-authored and illustrated by children – the poetry in *Through My Eyes* has brought joy to readers all over the country. There is space for young authors to write their own poems in the back of this book.

5 1/2" x 81/2" • 33 pages • $6.95
ISBN 1-879235-00-5
(WA State tax – $.60)